AF471676

Philo of Alexandria

On Rewards And Punishments

'The Early Jewish writers Series'

This is a publication of:
New Apostolic Bible Covenant ®
"Nova Vulgate Foederis Apostolicam"
MMXII-MMXIX

ISBN: 978-0-244-19340-9
1st Edition June 2019

Book designer: Apostle Horn
Design cover and composition: Apostle Horn
Source cover photo: https://www.jw.org/en/publications/books/true-faith/abraham-father-of-faith/

On Rewards And Punishments

Index:

Preface:

Philo of Alexandria (/ˈfaɪloʊ/; Greek: Φίλων, Philōn; Hebrew:ידידיה הכהן, Yedidia (Jedediah) HaCohen; c. 25 BCE – c. 50 CE), also called **Philo Judaeus**, was a Hellenistic Jewish philosopher who lived in Alexandria, in the Roman province of Egypt. Philo used philosophical allegory to attempt to fuse and harmonize Greek philosophy with Jewish philosophy. His method followed the practices of both Jewish exegesis and Stoic philosophy. His allegorical exegesis was important for several Christian Church Fathers, but he has barely any reception history within Rabbinic Judaism. He believed that literal interpretations of the Hebrew Bible would stifle humanity's view and perception of a God too complex and marvelous to be understood in literal human terms. Some scholars hold that his concept of the Logos as God's creative principle influenced early Christology. Other scholars, however, deny direct influence but say both Philo and Early Christianity borrow from a common source. The few biographical details known about Philo are found in his own works, especially in Legatio ad Gaium (Embassy to Gaius) of which only two of the original five volumes survive, and in Josephus. The only event in his life that can be decisively dated is his participation in the embassy to Rome in 40 CE. He represented the Alexandrian Jews before Roman Emperor Caligula because of civil strife between the Alexandrian Jewish and Greek communities. We find a brief reference to Philo by the 1st-century Jewish historian Josephus. In Antiquities of the Jews, Josephus tells of Philo's selection by the Alexandrian Jewish community as their principal representative before the Roman emperor Gaius Caligula. He says that Philo agreed to represent the Alexandrian Jews in regard to civil disorder that had developed between the Jews and the Greeks in Alexandria, Egypt. Josephus also tells us that Philo was skilled in philosophy, and that he was brother to an official called Alexander the alabarch. According to Josephus, Philo and the larger Jewish community refused to treat the emperor as a god, to erect statues in honor of the emperor, and to build altars and temples to the emperor. Josephus says Philo believed that God actively supported this refusal.

[source; https://en.wikipedia.org/wiki/Philo]

Intro;

The treatise begins with some remarks on the scheme on which Moses constructed his law book and how it was observed by some and disregarded by others. Coming to the main subject of the rewards for obedience and punishments for disobedience he notes that those described in the history may be classified under individuals, houses or groups, cities, countries and nations, and larger regions. We take the rewards to individuals and start with the less perfect Trinity, Enos, Enoch and Noah, who exemplify respectively hopefulness, repentance and justice. Hope is the motive of all human effort and hope in God is its only true form. Enos the hoper was rewarded with a name which means that he is a true man. Enoch's repentance is rewarded by his "transference" away from the common herd to the isolation which the converted need. Noah the just was saved from the flood and made the founder of renewed mankind. The second Trinity, Abraham, Isaac and Jacob, represent the true religion which despises vanity. Abraham the Taught learnt to believe in God and his reward was faith. Isaac the Self-taught instinctively rejoiced in all God's dispensations and his reward was joy. Jacob the Practiser sought to see God, not merely to infer him from his works, and his reward was the vision indicated by his name of Israel and also the spiritual qualities signified in the "numbing of the broad part." These lessons are recapitulated. But we must not forget Moses and his fourfold reward of kingship, lawgiving, prophecy and priesthood. We pass on to rewards to "houses." Abraham and Isaac had families which contained some unworthy members: Jacob's children alone as a body were qualified for the reward, namely the privilege of founding the twelve tribes which expanded into a great nation; incidentally we may draw a philosophical lesson from the three families as types of the children or qualities shown by the three types of soul. We then turn to the punishments of which only two examples are given in what has come down to us. First, for individuals we have Cain, whose punishment was to be ever dying, never dead, carrying on an existence from which joy and pleasure have been eliminated and in which not only permanent grief but fear of what is coming are perpetually present. For houses we have the revolt of the Levites under Korah. When the discourse, as we have it, is resumed we have come to the blessings promised in the law to the righteous. The first is victory over enemies, but before discussing who these enemies are he urges the necessity of not merely hearing but carrying out the law. The enemies are of two kinds, wild beasts and men; when men become what they should be, the beasts will also be tamed and men will eschew war with each other. War will either never come or if some still are mad enough to attack, they will be routed at once, and good government will be established. The second blessing is wealth, and many passages are cited which describe the abundance that is to be. The third is long life, and to this is appended the thought that the true long life is the good life, to which God may recall the human soul even as he promises to recall the repentant exiles. These four are external blessings; for the body there is promised the exemption from disease in which the good mind can rest and think. He then turns to punishment or curses, all of which closely follow Leviticus and Deuteronomy. The first is famine, drought and destruction of every kind of crop by nature if not by enemy, followed by all the horrors of cannibalism, miseries which they will be unable to escape by suicide; enslavement with all its miseries; a curse resting not only on the land and fruits but on all undertakings; bodily diseases of every kind; the terrors of war, panic, wild beasts, destruction of cities and finally utter despair. Meanwhile the proselytes will prosper, thus teaching the lesson that it is not race but obedience which brings salvation. He then descants on the Sabbaths which according to Leviticus the desolate land will enjoy. It had been wronged by the neglect of the sabbatical years, and will now take its rest and then after a while may produce a better race. This reminds him of the text "She that is desolate hath many children," a saying which can be applied allegorically to the converted soul which has been deserted by its vices and brings forth virtues. So much for the punishments, but there is also the promise of restoration to the penitent and a renewal of the national life in greater prosperity than ever; the curses will be turned upon the persecutors, who will find that their victory was transient and that the race which they despised had still a seed from which new life would spring.

On Rewards And Punishments

Chapter 1.
We find, then, that in the sacred oracles delivered by the prophet Moses, there are three separate characters; for a portion of them relates to the creation of the world, a portion is historical, and the third portion is legislative. Now the creation of the world is related throughout with exceeding beauty and in a manner admirably suited to the dignity of God, taking its beginning in the account of the creation of the heaven, and ending with that of the formation of man; the first of which things is the most perfect of all imperishable things, and the other of all corruptible and perishable things. And the Creator, connecting together immortal and mortal things at the creation, made the world, making what he had already created the dominant parts, and what he was about to create the subject parts. The historical part is a record of the lives of different wicked and virtuous men, and of the rewards, and honours, and punishments set apart for each class in each generation. The legislative part is sub-divided into two sections, one of which has a more general object proposed to it, laying down accordingly a few general comprehensive laws; the other part consists of special and particular ordinances. And the general heads of these special ordinances are ten, which are said not to have been delivered to the people by an interpreter, but to have been fashioned in the lofty region of the air, and to have been connected by a rational distinctness and utterance. While the others, I mean the particular and minute laws, were delivered by the prophet. And as, in my former treatises, I have dwelt upon each of these to as great an extent as the time permitted me, and as I have also enlarged upon all the different virtues which the lawgiver has assigned to peace and war, I will now proceed in regular order to mention the rewards which have been proposed for virtuous men, and the punishments threatened to the wicked; for, after he had trained all those who are living under his constitution and laws by gentle precepts, and admonitions, and expectations, and subsequently by more several threats and warning, he summoned them all to hear the promulgation of the law; and they all, coming as to a sacred meeting, displayed their own eager choice and approbation of those laws in such a way as to give a most convincing proof of their truth. And then some of them were found to be diligent labourers in the practice of virtue, not disappointing the good hopes which were formed of them, nor dishonouring the laws which were their instructors. Others were found to be unmanly, and effeminate, and cowardly, out of the innate weakness and imbecility of their souls, who, fainting before any real danger or trouble came upon them, disgraced themselves and became the ridicule of the spectators. On which account the one class received decisions in their favour, and proclamations in their honour, and all such rewards as are usually given to conquerors; while the others departed not only without the garlands of victory, but even after having sustained a most disgraceful defeat,

more grievous than any which befalls a man in the gymnastic contests. For there the bodies, indeed, of the athletes are overthrown, but so that they can be easily raised again; but in this case it is the whole life which falls, which, when once it is overthrown, it is scarcely possible to raise again. And our lawgiver announces a very suitable arrangement and appointment of privileges and honours for the one; and, on the contrary, of punishments for the others, as affecting individuals, and houses, and cities, and countries, and nations, and vast regions of the earth.

Chapter 2.

And, first of all, we must investigate the subject of honours, since that is both more profitable and more pleasant to hear of, taking our commencement from the particular instances of individuals. The Greeks say that in ancient times the famous Triptolemus was raised aloft and borne on winged dragons, and that while flying along in this manner he sowed the grains of wheat over the whole of the earth, in order that, instead of eating acorns, the human race might for the future have wholesome, and advantageous, and most pleasant food. This story, then, like many other tales, being, as it were, a fabulous fiction, may well be left to those who are accustomed to study sophistry rather than wisdom, and juggling tricks in preference to the truth; for originally and simultaneously with the first creation of the universe, God supplied all living creatures with necessary food, producing it out of the earth, and, above all things, providing the race of mankind with all that was requisite, to whom also he gave the supremacy over every animal born of the earth. For, among the works of the Deity, there is nothing posthumous, but all those things which appear to be brought to perfection at a subsequent time by the care, and diligence, and skill of men are in all cases previously produced in a half-finished state by the provident care of nature, so that it is not a wholly absurd statement that all learning is only recollection. However, these questions may be postponed for subsequent discussion. But we must now consider that most necessary of all things, the sowing of seed, which the Creator has sown in a very excellent soil, namely, in the rational soul. Now, of this the most important seed is hope, the fountain of all men's lives; for it is by the hope of gain that the money-changer applies himself to many kinds of traffic; and it is through hope of a favourable voyage that the sailor passes over long seas; and it is from hope of glory that the ambitious man applies himself to public affairs, and to the superintendance of the commonwealth and matters of state. It is through hope of decisions in their favour and of crowns, that those who exercise their bodies in athletic labours enter the gymnastic contests. Hope is the source of all happiness; hope excites those persons who are filled with an admiration of virtue to study philosophy, under the idea that by her means they will be able to obtain a clear sight of the nature of all existing things, and to do things which are in accordance with and consistent with the perfection of those who most excellent modes of life--and contemplative and the practical, which he who attains to is at once truly happy. Now some persons have either, like enemies, stifled and destroyed all the seeds of hope by kindling all the vices in the soul, or else, like persons ignorant of and indifferent to the skill of the husbandman, they have allowed them to perish through neglect. There are also some persons who, appearing to be diligent husbandmen, but who yet, esteeming self-love above piety, have attributed the causes of their successes to themselves. And all these men are very blameable, and he alone is worthy of being accepted who attributes his hope to God, both as being the author of his birth and as being alone able to keep him free from injury and free from utter destruction. What reward, then, is assigned to the man who is crowned as conqueror in this contest? Man is a compound animal, made up of a mortal and immortal nature, not being the same with nor yet entirely different from the one who has obtained the prize. This man the Chaldaeans name Enos, but this name, when translated into the Grecian language, means "a man," he having received the common name of the whole race for his own name, as an especial honour; as if it was not right for any one to be considered as a man at all who does not hope in God.

Chapter 3.

And after the victory of hope there is another contest in which repentance contends for the prize; having, indeed, no share in that nature which is invincible, and which never changes its purpose, and which is always of the same character, entertaining the same disposition, but which is on a sudden seized with an admiration for and love of the better part, and which is anxious to leave the covetousness and injustice in which it has been bred up, and to go over to moderation and justice, and the other virtues; for these are twofold prizes, which are proposed for twofold successes, first of all for the abandonment of what is disgraceful, and, secondly, for the choice of what is excellent; and the prizes are a departure from home, and solitude. For Moses says, with reference to one who fled from the audacious innovations of the body, and who came over to the interest of the soul, "He was not found because God changed his Place;" (Genesis 5:24.} and by this enigmatical expression the two things are clearly intimated, the migration by the change of place, and the solitude by his not being found. And very appropriately is this stated; for if in real truth man had resolved at all times to show himself really superior to the passions, despising all pleasures and all appetites, then he would require to prepare himself diligently, fleeing without ever turning his head round, and forsaking his home, and his country, and his relations, and his friends; for familiar custom is an attractive thing, so that there is reason to fear that if a man remains behind he may be taken prisoner, being caught by such powerful charms all round, the appearances of which will again rouse up the disgraceful though at present dormant appetites for evil pursuits, and will restore to vitality those recollections which it was creditable to have forgotten. Accordingly, many persons have become corrected and improved by migrations from their native land, having been cured by such means of their frenzied and wicked desires, by reason of the sight no longer being able to furnish to the passion the images of pleasure. For in consequence of the separation which has taken place, this passion has only a vacuum through which to rove, since there is no longer any object present by which it can be inflamed. And if it does rise up and quit its former abode, still let it avoid the assemblies of the multitude, embracing solitude; for there are snares in a foreign land resembling those, which are found in a man's own country into which those men must fall who are careless and do not look before them, and who rejoice in the society of the multitude; for the multitude is a very concentration of every thing that is irregular, disorderly, improper, and blameable, with which it is a most mischievous thing for the man who is now for the first time passing over to the ranks of virtue to proceed. For as the bodies of those men who are only just beginning to recover from a long attack of sickness are very subject to a relapse; so the soul which is just recovering its health finds its intellectual vigour weak and wavering, so that there is room to apprehend that the evil passions may return which were wont to be excited in it by a habit of living in the society of inconsiderate men.

Chapter 4.

Then, after these contests in which repentance is concerned, he proposes a third class of prizes, relating to justice, which every one who practises obtains a twofold reward; in the first place, that of preservation at the time of general destruction; and secondly, that of being the steward and guardian of every description of animal which is coupled in pairs for the purpose of raising a second stock instead of that which from time to time perishes; for the Creator provided that the same being should be both the end of the generation which is condemned and the beginning of that which is irreproachable, teaching those who say that the world is destitute of all providence by works and not by words, that in accordance with the law which he promulgated and established in the nature of things, all the innumerable multitudes of men which live in obedience to injustice are not to be compared to one single individual who lives as a follower of justice. Now this man the Greeks call Deucalion, but the Chaldaeans name him Noah; and it was in his time that the great deluge took place. And after this triad there was a second triad still more holy and more pious, of one family. For father, and son, and grandson all directed all their views to the same end of life, namely, to please the Creator and Father of the universe, despising all those objects which the generality of men admire; glory, and riches, and pleasure, and laughing at that pride which is continually being put together and set forth with all kinds of fictitious ornaments in order to deceive the spectators. This is that which makes gods of inanimate things, a great and almost impregnable fortification by the sophistries and manoeuvres of whom every city is allured, and since it takes especial hold on the souls of the young. For having entered into them it establishes itself and dwells in them from the earliest infancy to old age, subduing all those on whom God has not poured the beams of his truth. But pride is the adversary of truth, and is hard to be removed, though when it is subdued by a stronger power than itself then it does depart. And this class of men is small, indeed, in number; but in power it is very numerous and very great, so that even the whole circle of the earth cannot contain it. And it reaches even to heaven; for as it is possessed of an indescribable love of contemplation and of being always among divine objects, when it has thoroughly investigated and explained all that nature which is perceptible to the sight, it immediately proceeds onwards to that which is incorporeal and appreciable only by the intellect, without requiring the assistance of any one of the outward senses, indeed discarding even the irrational parts of the soul, and employing those parts only which are called mind and reason. Therefore, the first establisher of the sentiments devoted to God, namely, Abraham, the first person who passed over from pride to truth, employing that virtue which proceeds from instruction as a means towards perfection, chooses as his reward faith in God. And because he, by the innate goodness of his natural dispositions, had acquired a spontaneous, self-taught, and selfimplanted virtue, joy was given to him as a prize. Again, to his grandson, the meditator on and practiser of virtue, who attained to what was good by indefatigable and incessant labours, the crown which was given was the sight of God. And what can any one conceive to be either more useful or more respectable than to believe in God and throughout one's whole life to be continually rejoicing and beholding the living God?

Chapter 5.

And let us now perceive each of these things more accurately, without allowing ourselves to be led away by names, but investigating them in their inmost parts, and going deep into them with our minds. Therefore, he who has in all sincerity believed God has by so doing received a disbelief in all other things which are created and perishable, beginning with those things in himself which exalt themselves very highly, namely, reason and the outward sense. For each of these things has a private consistory and tribunal of its own, which is erected in the one in order to ensure the proper consideration of the objects appreciable only by the intellect, the end of which is truth; and in the other for the perception of visible things, the end of which is opinion. Therefore, the unstable, and erroneous, and untrustworthy character of opinion is plain from this circumstance; for it anchors upon images and probabilities. And every image is deceitful, exhibiting itself by a certain attractive similarity in lieu of the original thing itself. But reason, which is the leader of the outward sense, thinking that the decision about all things which are perceptible only by the intellect, and which are always the same and in the same condition, belongs to itself, is convicted of being in error on many points. For when it directs its view to particular instances which are innumerable, it finds itself powerless, and unequal to the task, and faints under it, like a wrestler who is stripped up by some more mighty power; but the man to whom it has been granted to see and thoroughly examine all corporeal and all incorporeal things, and to lean upon and to found himself upon God alone, with firm and steadfast reason and unalterable and sure confidence, is truly happy and blessed. After faith the next prize which is offered as destined for the man who acquires virtue by the gift of nature, as being victorious without a struggle, is joy. For this man is named as the Greeks would call him, Laughter, but as the Chaldaeans would entitle him, Isaac. And laughter is an emblem in the body of that unseen joy which exists in the mind. And joy is the most excellent and the most beautiful of all the pleasant affections of the mind, by means of which the whole soul is in every part entirely filled with cheerfulness, rejoicing in the Father and Creator of all men and things, namely, in God, and rejoicing also in those things which are done without wickedness, even though they may not be pleasant, as being done virtuously, and as contributing to the duration of the universe. For as in great and dangerous sicknesses a physician sometimes actually takes away parts of the body, aiming at ensuring the sound health of the rest, and as when storms arise the pilot often throws overboard the cargo, out of a prudent regard to the safety of the men sailing in the ship; and yet the physician is not blamed for the mutilation of the body, nor the pilot for the loss of the cargo, but on the contrary both of them are praised as having seen and ensured what was advantageous in preference to what was pleasant; so in the same manner we must always look with proper admiration at the nature of the entire universe, and we must be pleased with all things which are done in the world without intentional wickedness, inquiring not whether any thing has been done which is not altogether pleasant, but whether the world, like a city enjoying good laws, is guided and governed in a manner calculated to ensure its safety. This man, therefore, is happy in no less a degree than the one whom I mentioned before, inasmuch as he is free from all depression or melancholy, and as he enjoys a life exempt from sorrow and exempt from fear, having no connection, not even in a dream, with any painful or austere plans of life, because every part of his soul is wholly occupied by joy.

Chapter 6.

And next to the man who has acquired self-taught virtue, and who has availed himself of the riches of nature, the third person who is made perfect is the meditator on and practiser of virtue, who receives as his especial reward the sight of God; for as he has had experience of all the things which can occur in human life, and as he has attained to a most intimate understanding of them, and has shrunk from no labour and from no danger which might enable him to track out and overtake that most desirable thing, truth, he has found in connection with human life and with the human race a great deal of darkness both by land and sea, and in the air, and in the atmosphere. For the atmosphere and the whole of heaven has presented to him the appearance of night, since every nature which is discernible by the outward senses is indefinite; and what is indefinite is akin to and closely resembling darkness. Accordingly, he who had during the preceding periods of his life had the eyes of his soul closed, now began, though with difficulty, to open them for the continual labours which were before him, and to pierce through and dissipate the mist which had overshadowed him. For an incorporeal ray of light, purer than the atmosphere, suddenly beaming upon him, displayed to him the fact of the world appreciable only by the intellect being guided by a regular governor. But that governor or guider, being surrounded on all sides by unalloyed light, was difficult to be perceived and difficult to be understood by conjecture, since the power of sight was obscured by the brilliancy of those beams. But nevertheless the sight, although a great violence of fire was poured upon it, held out against it out of an immense desire of seeing what was before it. And the Father pitied its sincere desire and eagerness to see, and gave it power, and did not grudge the acuteness of the sight thus directed a perception of himself, as far at least as a created and mortal nature could attain to such a thing, not indeed such a perception as should show him what God is, but merely such as should prove to him that he exists; for even this, which is better than good, and more ancient than the unit, and more simple than one, cannot possibly be contemplated by any other being; because, in fact, it is not possible for God to be comprehended by any being but himself.

Chapter 7.

But the fact that he does exist, though it is comprehensible from the mere name of existence, is nevertheless not understood by every one, or at all events not in the best way by every one; but some men have expressly and wholly denied that there is any deity at all; while others have doubted and hesitated, as if they were unable to affirm with certainty whether he has any existence or not. Others again, who have more through habit than from any exertion of their reason, received ideas about the existence of God from those who have brought them up, have seemed to be pious by a sort of felicity of conjecture, if they have stamped their piety with an impression of superstition. But if any men, by a great depth of real knowledge, have been able to represent to themselves the Creator and Governor of this universe, they, according to the common phrase, have advanced upwards from below; for having entered into this world as into a city regulated by admirable laws, and having beheld the earth consisting of mountains, and of plains, and full of seed-crops, and of trees, and of fruits, and also of all kinds of animals; and beholding also seas, and ports, and lakes, and rivers of all sorts, whether proceeding from winter floods, or from everlasting springs, diffused over the surface of it, and the admirable temperature of the breezes and of the atmosphere, and the harmonious changes and well-ordered revolutions of the seasons of the year, and beyond all these things, the sun and moon, the planets and fixed stars, and the whole heaven, and all the host of heaven in its proper arrangement, and, in fact, the whole real world revolving in admirable order and regularity: admiring, and being struck with awe and amazement at these things, they are come to form notions consistent with what they behold, that all these beautiful things, excessive as they are, and of such admirable arrangement and contrivance, were not produced spontaneously but were the work of some maker, the Creator of the whole world, and therefore that there must of necessity be a superintending providence. For it is a law of nature, that the Creator must take care of what he has created. But these admirable men, so superior to all others, have, as I said, raised themselves upwards from below, ascending as if by some ladder reaching to heaven, so as, through the contemplation of his works, to form a conjectural conception of the Creator by a probable train of reasoning. And if any persons have been able to comprehend him by himself, without employing any other reasonings as assistants towards their perception of him, they deserve to be recorded as holy and genuine servants of his, and sincere worshippers of God. In this company is the man who in the Chaldaean language is denominated Israel, but in the Greek "seeing God;" not meaning by this expression seeing what kind of being God is, for that is impossible, as I have said before, but seeing that he really does exist; not having learnt this fact from any one else, nor from anything on earth, nor from anything in heaven, nor from any one of the elements, nor from anything compounded of them, whether mortal or immortal, but being instructed in the fact by God himself, who is willing to reveal his own existence to his suppliant. And how this impression was made, it is worth while to see by the observation of some similitude. Take this sun, which is perceptible by our outward senses, do we see it by any other means than by the aid of the sun? And do we see the stars by any other light than that of the stars? And, in short, is not all light seen in consequence of light? And in the same manner God, being his own light, is perceived by himself alone, nothing and no other being co-operating with or assisting him, or being at all able to contribute to the pure comprehension of his existence; therefore those persons are mere guessers who are anxious to contemplate the uncreated God through the medium of the things which he created, acting like those persons who seek to ascertain the nature of the unit through the number two, when they ought, on the other hand, to employ the investigation of the unit itself to ascertain the nature of the number two; for the unit is the first principle. But these men have arrived at the real truth, who form their ideas of God from God, of light from light.

Chapter 8.

We have now described the greatest prize of all: but in addition to these prizes, the meditator on virtue receives another prize, not well-sounding indeed as to name, but very excellent to be conceived of; and this prize is called "the torpor of breadth," speaking figuratively. Now by breadth haughtiness and arrogance are typified; the soul, in those conditions, pouring forth an immoderate effusion over objects which are not desirable: and by torpor is typified the contraction of conceit, an elated and puffed-up thing. But nothing is so expedient, as that unrestrained and unlimited impulses should be repressed and reduced to torpor, through the spirit of the mind being extinguished: so that the immoderate violence of the passions having become enfeebled, it may give breadth to the better part of the soul. And we must also consider how exceedingly suitable a prize has thus been assigned to each of the three individuals; for to him who has been made perfect by education, faith is given as his reward; since it is necessary that he who learns must trust the man who teaches him in the matters concerning which he is instructing him; for it is difficult, or rather I might say impossible, for a man to be instructed who distrusts his teacher. Again: to him who arrives at virtue by his own good natural disposition, joy is given; for a good natural disposition is a thing to be rejoiced at, and so are the gifts of nature; since the mind derives enjoyment from all displays of acuteness and felicitous inventions, by which it finds the object which it is seeking without trouble; as if there was some prompter within enriching it with inventions; for the prompt discovery of matters previously, not certainly understood, is a subject of joy. Again: to him who has acquired wisdom by meditation and practice, sight is given. For after the practical life of youth comes the contemplative life of old age, which is the most excellent and the most sacred, which God has sent down from above to take its place in the stern like a pilot, and has given the helm into his hand as being able to guide the course of all earthly things; for without contemplation based on knowledge, there is nothing whatever that is good done.

Chapter 9.

Having thus mentioned one man of each class, since I am anxious not to be prolix, I will proceed to what comes next in the order of discussion. Now, this man was proclaimed as conqueror, and crowned as such in the sacred contests. And when I speak of sacred contests, I do not mean those which are accounted such by other nations, for they are in reality unholy, affixing, as they do, rewards and honours to acts of violence, and insolence, and injustice, instead of the very extremity of punishment, which of right belongs to them: but I mean rather such as the soul is by nature formed to go through, which, by means of prudence, drives away folly and wicked cunning, and by temperance drives away prodigality and stinginess, and by courage drives away both rashness and cowardice, and the other vices which are in direct opposition to the respective virtues, and which are of no use either to themselves or to any one else; therefore all the virtues are presented as virgins. And the most excellent of all, having taken the post of leader as if in a chorus, is piety and righteousness, which Moses, the interpreter of the will of God, possessed in a most eminent degree. On which account, besides an innumerable host of other circumstances which are recorded of him in the accounts which have come down to us of his life, he has received also four most especial prizes, in being invested with sovereign power, with the office of lawgiver, with the power of prophecy, and with the office of high priest. For he was a king, not indeed according to the usual fashion with soldiers and arms, and forces of fleets, and infantry, and cavalry, but as having been appointed by God, with the free consent of the people who were to be governed by him, and who wrought in his subjects a willingness to make such a voluntary choice. For he is the only king of whom we have any mention as being neither a speaker nor one frequently heard, nor possessed of wealth or riches, since he was anxious rather about the wealth which sees than about that which is blind, and, if one is to speak the truth without any concealment, one who looked upon the inheritance of God as his peculiar property. And this same man was likewise a lawgiver; for a king must of necessity both command and forbid, and law is nothing else but a discourse which enjoins what is right and forbids what is not right; but since it is uncertain what is expedient in each separate case (for we often out of ignorance command what is not right to be done, and forbid what is right), it was very natural for him also to receive the gift of prophecy, in order to ensure him against stumbling; for a prophet is an interpreter, God from within prompting him what he ought to say; and with God nothing is blameable. In the fourth place he received the high priesthood, by means of which he, prophesying in accordance with knowledge, worships the living God, and by which also he will bring before him in a propitiating manner, the thanksgivings of his subjects when they do well, and their prayers and supplications if at any time they are unfortunate; now since all these things belong to one class, they ought to be held together and united by mutual bonds, and to be perceived in the same man, since he who is deficient in any one of the four is imperfect in his authority, as he is consequently invested with but a crippled authority over the common interests.

Chapter 10.

We have now thus spoken at sufficient length concerning the rewards proposed for each individual man: but rewards are also offered to whole houses, and to very numerous families. When the nation was originally divided into twelve tribes, there were at once appointed patriarchs equal in number to the tribes, being not merely of one house or family, but connected by a still more genuine relationship: for they were all brothers having one and the same father; and the father and grandfather of these men were, with their father, the original founders of the whole nation. Therefore the first man who forsook pride and came over to truth, and who despised the jugglery of the Chaldaic branches of learning, because of that more perfect vision which had been granted to him, after having seen which he was so captivated that he followed the vision, just as they say that wire is attracted by the magnet, becoming instead of a sophist which he had been before a wise man in consequence of instruction--he had many children: but they were not all virtuous, though there was one who was utterly blameless, to whom he bound the cables of his whole race, and thus brought them to a safe anchorage. Again his son who had acquired spontaneous and self-taught wisdom had two sons, one a wild and untameable man, full of anger and desire, and one in short who raised up the irrational part of his soul as a fortification against the rational part; but the other a mild and gentle follower and worker of virtue, placed in the more excellent class of equality and simplicity, the very champion of reason and declared enemy of folly: he is the third of the founders of his race, a man with many sons, and the only one truly happy in this children, being free from all injury in every part of his family, and like a fortunate husbandman seeing all his seed in a state of safety, and well cultivated, and bearing fruit.

Chapter 11.

And every one of these three individuals has in the account which we have received of him a figurative meaning concealed below it, which we must now consider. Now the moment that any one is taught anything, it happens to him to forsake ignorance and to come over the knowledge; and ignorance is a thing of a multiform character: on this account the first of the three is said to have had many children, but not to have thought any one of them worthy for him to call his son, except one: for in a manner he who learns discards the offspring of ignorance, and repudiates them as inimical and hostile to him. Now by nature all we who are men, before the reason that is in us is brought to perfection, live on the borders between virtue and vice, without ever inclining as yet to either side: but when the mind, beginning to put forth its wings, sees an appearance of the good with its whole soul, impressing it in all its parts, it immediately bursts through all restraint, and being borne on wings rushes towards it, leaving behind the kindred evil which was born with it, which it flees from, proceeding in the other direction without ever turning back: this is what he intends to imply by an enigmatical expression when he says that the man who was endowed by nature with a good disposition had two sons, twins: for every man has at the beginning simultaneously with his birth, a soul which is pregnant with twins, namely, good and evil, bearing the impression of both of them: but when it receives the blessed and happy part, then by the force of one single attraction it inclines to the good, never once leaning towards the other side, and never even wavering so as to appear to be balancing between the two. But that soul which besides having a good natural disposition has also received a good education, and has been trained by the third mentioned person in the meditations of virtue, so that none of them float at random on the surface, but that they are all firmly glued and fixed in their places, as if united by some compact sinews, acquires health and acquires power, which are followed by a good complexion, owing to modesty, and also good health and beauty. And thus the soul becoming a perfect company of virtues, by means of these three most excellent patronesses, nature, instruction, and meditation, and not having left one single spot in itself empty, so as to allow of the entrance of anything else, engenders perfect number, namely, two lots of sons, of six in each, being a representation and imitation of the circle of the zodiac, in order to the improvement of everything in them: this is the family exempt from all injury, being continually devoted to the study of the holy scriptures, both in their literal sense and also in the allegories figuratively contained in them: which received as a prize, as I have said before, the supreme authority over each of the tribes of the nation. Of this house therefore, as it increased and became very populous in process of time, well regulated cities were founded, being schools of wisdom, and justice, and holiness, in which also the means of acquiring all other virtue was investigated in a grave manner suited to the importance of the subject.

Chapter 12.

Therefore those rewards which were thus long since assigned to the good, both publicly and privately, have now been described though somewhat in outline, but sufficiently to enable anyone to comprehend with tolerable ease what has been omitted. We must now proceed in regular order to consider in turn the punishments appointed for the wicked, speaking of them in a somewhat general way since the time does not allow of my enumerating all the particular instances. Now there was at the very beginning of the world when the race of men had not as yet multiplied, a fratricide: this is the first man who ever was under a curse; the first man who imprinted on the pure earth the unprecedented pollution of human blood; the first man who checked the fertility of the earth which was previously blooming, and producing all kinds of animals, and plants, and flourishing with every kind of productiveness; the first man who introduced destruction as a rival against creation, death against life, sorrow against joy, and evil against good. What then could possibly have been inflicted upon him, which would have been an adequate punishment for him, who thus in one single action left no description of violence and impiety unperformed? Perhaps some one will say he should have been put to death at once; this is a human mode of reasoning, fit for one who does not consider the great tribunal of all for men look upon death as the extreme limit of all punishments, but in the view of the divine tribunal it is scarcely the beginning of them. Since then the action of this man was a novel one, it was necessary that a novel punishment should be devised for him; and what was it? That he should live continually dying, and that he should in a manner endure an undying and never ending death; for there are two kinds of death; the one that of being dead, which is either good or else a matter of indifference; the other that of dying, which is in every respect an evil; and the more protracted the dying the more intolerable the evil. Consider now then how it is that death can be said to be never ending in this man's case; since there are four different affections to which the soul is liable, two of them being conversant with good either present or future, namely, pleasure and desire; and two with evil either present or expected, namely, sorrow and fear; it cuts up the pair of those which are conversant with good by the roots, in order that the man may never receive pleasure from any accident of fortune, nor ever feel a desire even for anything pleasant; and it leaves him only those affections conversant about evil, sorrow without any mixture of cheerfulness, and unmingled fear, for the scripture says: {Genesis 4:14.} that God laid a curse upon the fratricide, so that he should be continually groaning and trembling. Moreover he put a mark upon him, that he might never be pitied by any one, so that he might not die once, but might, as I have said before, pass all his time in dying, amid griefs, and pains, and incessant calamities; and what is most grievous of all, might have a feeling of his own miseries, and be afflicted both with the evils which were before him, and also from a foresight of the number of misfortunes which were constantly impending over him, which nevertheless he was unable to guard against, since hope was wholly taken from him, which God has implanted in the race of mankind, in order that thus, having an innate comfort in themselves, they might feel their sorrows relieved, provided they had not committed any inexpiable crimes. Therefore, as a man who is being carried away by a torrent shudders at the nearest waves by which he is being hurried away, and still more at those coming upon him from above, since the one is continually and incessantly propelling him forward with violence, but the other being raised above him threatens to overwhelm him utterly, so in the same manner those evils which are present are grievous, but those which proceed from fear of the future are more grievous still; for fear continually supplies sorrowful feelings as from an everlasting spring.

Chapter 13.

These punishments, then, are those which were decided on to be inflicted on the first slayer of his brother. But others were also appointed for households which had entered into any conspiracy to unite in crime. And there were some men appointed to be keepers of the temple and ministers in the sacred offices, classed as a kind of door-keepers. These men, being wholly filled with unreasonable pride, rose up in rebellion against the priests, desiring to appropriate their honours and privileges to themselves. And, having elected as chief of their conspiracy the eldest of their body, who also, with a few of those who joined in this audacious folly, was the leader of the whole enterprise, they left the outer courts and precincts of the tabernacle and entered into the most holy places, expelling those who, by the oracular commands of God, had been thought worthy of the priesthood. Therefore, as was natural, a great confusion spread among the whole multitude, in consequence of things being disturbed which never ought to have been moved, and of the laws being openly violated and all the ordinances for the regular service of the temple being thrown into confusion by wicked disobedience, at which the governor and president of the nation was indignant. And, at first, displaying a stern disposition, though without any anger (for he was the meekest of men and by nature incapable of anger), he endeavoured by arguments to persuade them to alter their conduct, and not to transgress the bounds laid down for them, nor to seek to overturn the ordinances established with respect to holy and consecrated things on which the hopes of the whole nation depended. But when he would not succeed in the least, but found that the people were deaf to all his entreaties, since they looked upon him as wholly under the influence of domestic affection and thought that it was on that account that he had made his brother high priest, and had given the inferior priesthood to his nephews, he still was not so much indignant at that, though it was a shocking thing, as at this other all terrible idea that they were imputing to him a contempt for the sacred oracles, in accordance with which the election of priests had taken place:{Numbers 16:1.}{there appears to be a considerable hiatus in the text here.}

Chapter 14.

And there is a distinct evidence in confirmation of what I have now said recorded in the sacred scriptures; because, in the first place, the sacred historian records the prayers which he commonly calls blessings. "If,"{Deuteronomy 30:10.} says he, "you keep the commandments of God and are obedient to his injunctions, and receive what is said to you, not merely so far as to listen to them, but also to fulfil them by the actions of your lives, you shall have as a first reward victory over your enemies; for the commandments are not burdensome or too weighty for the ability of you who are to live by them to obey, nor is the good which is promised to you removed to any distance, ether beyond the sea, or at the furthest extremities of the country, so as to require a long and painful journey to avail yourselves of it." Nor did the lawgiver at once set out on his departure from earth to heaven, so that no one else being raised on high and borne aloft on wings could attain to the obedience which he enjoined; but the obedience remained near and very close to men, being fixed separately in three parts of us, in the mouth, and heart, and hands; that is to say, in the speech, and designs, and actions of every one. For if such as the designs are, such also are the speeches; and such as the words spoken, such also are the actions; and if these things are bound up with each other, reciprocally preceding and following one another through the indissoluble bonds of harmony; then happiness prevails, and this is the truest wisdom and prudence. For wisdom has reference to the service of God, and prudence to the regulation of human life. Therefore, as long as the commandments conveyed in the laws are only spoken, they meet with but little or no acceptance; but when words in proper consistency and conformity with them are added to them in all the pursuits of life, then those commandments, being brought forth as it were from deep darkness to light, will shine forth in all respectability and glory for when of those who are naturally envious, would hesitate to say that this is the only wise and truly learned race of men, which has the sense not to leave the divine commands destitute of and unattended by corresponding actions, but which takes care to fulfil the words with praiseworthy actions? This class of men lives not far from God, keeping always before its eyes the beautiful things of heaven, and being guided in all its ways by heavenly love; so that if any one were to inquire of what character a great nation is, one might very properly answer it is a nation whose most sacred prayers God hears, and to whose invocations, proceeding as they do from a pure conscience, he gladly draws near.

Chapter 15.

But since there are also two classes of enemies--the one being men, who are so deliberately, out of covetousness; the other being beasts, who are not so out of any deliberate purpose, or through study, but as being endowed with a nature utterly alien to ours--we must proceed to speak of them both in turn, and we will take, in the first place, the beasts which are our natural enemies; for these are hostile not to one city, or to one nation, but to the whole race of mankind, and that too not for any definite or limited period of time, but for an indefinite and illimitable eternity. Of these some fear man as their master, and crouch beneath him with an angry fear; others, again, being bold and fearless, watch their opportunity and are the first to begin the warfare and attack him; if they are weaker than he, by an ambush; and if they are stronger, openly. For this war is one which admits of no truce and of no termination, but is like that existing between the wolves and the sheep, and between all wild beasts, whether living in the water or on the land, and men; and no mortal can terminate it, but only the one uncreated God, when he selects some persons as worthy to be the saviours of their race; men who are peaceful, indeed, in disposition, fond of unanimity and fellowship with others, with whom envy has either absolutely never had any connection at all, or else it has speedily departed from them; and these men have determined to throw all their own private good things into the common stock for the use and enjoyment of all. For if this good should ever at any future time shine upon the world, so that we may be able to see the time in which the savage animals shall become manageable, long before that the wild passions in the soul will be tamed, and it is not possible to imagine a greater blessing than that; for is it not a piece of absolute folly to imagine that we can ever avoid injuries from wild beasts which are outside, while we are continually training up the passions within ourselves to a terrible degree of savageness? On which account we must not despair that when the passions of our mind are tamed and subdued, then the wild beasts also will be broken in. Then it seems to me that bears, and lions, and leopards, and those beasts which are found only in India, elephants and tigers, and all other animals whose courage and strength are invincible, will change from their solitary and unsociable habits, and adopt a more gregarious life, and, by a gradual imitation of those animals which live in troops, will become softened and accustomed to the sight of men, being no longer in a constant state of excitement and fury against him, but rather feeling awe of him as their ruler and natural master, and will behave with proper respect to him; and some of them, with an exceeding greatness of tameness and affection for their master, like Maltese dogs, will even fawn upon them and wag their tails with a cheerful motion. Then the species of scorpions, and serpents, and other reptiles will keep their venom inoperative; and the Egyptian river will produce those animals, which are at present carnivorous and which feed on man, called crocodiles and hippopotami, in a tame and gentle condition; and the sea too will produce innumerable kinds of animals, among all of which the virtuous man will be sacred and unhurt, since God honours virtue and has given it immunity from all designs against it as a proper reward.

<u>Chapter 16.</u>

Thus, then, the most ancient war, both in point of time and in nature, will be put an end to, when all the wild beasts will be tamed and will have altered their dispositions so as to become manageable. But the more modern war, which has arisen out of the deliberate purposes of men from their covetousness, will be likewise easily put an end to, as it appears to me, since men will be ashamed to be seen to be more savage than even the brute beasts, after they have escaped all injury and damage from them; for it will naturally appear a most shameful thing for venomous, carnivorous, man-devouring, unsociable, ferocious animals to have become friendly to man, changing to a peaceful disposition, and for man, who is by nature a gentle animal, with a natural inclination to sociality and unanimity, to renounce peace and seek the destruction of his fellows. Therefore, says the lawgiver, peace shall never come at all into the country of the pious, but shall fall to pieces of itself, and shall be dashed to pieces against itself, when the enemies perceive against what fierce and invincible enemies the contest is, and employ against them the irresistible alliance of justice; for virtue is a great, and dignified, and very venerable thing, and is by itself, when in tranquillity, able to alleviate the attacks of great evils. And even if some men are in their frenzy driven to quarrel, indulging their spontaneous and implacable desire for war, until indeed they are actually engaged, they will, being full of confidence, behave with great insolence, but after they have once come to a regular contest they will then find that they have made an empty boast, and that they are unable to gain the victory; for as they will be repelled by force equal to their own, {Leviticus 26:8.} or even more powerful still, they will flee in great confusion, a hundred fleeing before five, and a host of ten thousand before a hundred men, and those who had come by one road fleeing by a great number. Some will even flee when no one pursues at all except fear, turning their backs towards the enemy, so as to afford a full mark for shooting, so that it will be very easy for the whole army to fall, being slain to a man; for a man will come forth, {Numbers 24:7.} says the word of God, leading a host and warring furiously, who will subdue great and populous nations, God sending that assistance which is suitable for pious men; and this assistance is an intrepid hardihood of soul, and an irresistible strength of body, either of which things is formidable to the enemy, and if both qualities are united they are completely invincible. Moreover he says, "That some of the enemy will be unworthy of being defeated and of perishing by the hands of men, to which he will oppose swarms of wasps, {Exodus 23:28.} who shall fight for the pious, so as to overwhelm their enemies with shameful destruction; and he predicts, that he will not only always firmly retain the bloodless victory thus gained, but that he will also have an irresistible power of dominion, so as to be able to benefit the people subject to him, who may become so, whether out of good will, or out of fear, or out of shame; for he will have in him three things of the greatest importance, all contributing greatly to rendering his authority indestructible, namely, dignity, and terror, and beneficence, by means of which qualities the ends above-mentioned will be gained; for dignity causes respect, and terror causes fear, and beneficence causes good will; which, when they are mixed together, and adapted, and united in the soul, render subjects obedient to their rulers.

Chapter 17.

These, then, are the first things which he says will happen to those who obey God, and who at all times and in all places observe his commandments, and who adapt them to every part of their lives, so that no one going astray under the influence of disease may wander from them. The second thing is wealth, which must of necessity follow peace and authority; but the simple wealth of nature is food and shelter, and food is bread and water from the spring, which are both diffused over every part of the habitable world; but of shelter there are two kinds, first of all clothes, and secondly a house, on account of the injuries which result from exposure to cold and heat; each of which protections, if any one chooses to discard superfluous and excessive extravagance, is very easily provided. But those who admire what has been described above, having rather a desire for the gifts of nature than for those of vain opinion, devoting themselves to frugality, and simplicity, and temperance, will have a great abundance and means for all kinds of delicate living without any labour or study; for wealth will come to those who know how to use it in a befitting manner, as to those who are at the same time the most proper, and, in fact, the most nearly related to it and thoroughly worthy of it, gladly fleeing from all association with intemperate and insolent men, that it may not pass by those persons whose existence is a common benefit to mankind, and supply those who live to the injury of their neighbours; for there is a passage in the word of God, {Leviticus 26:3.} that, "on those who observe the sacred commands of God, the heaven will shower down seasonable rains, and the earth will bring forth for them abundance of all kinds of fruits, the champaign country producing crops from seed, and the mountainous country fruit from trees;" and that no period will ever be left entirely destitute of benefits for them, but that they shall without interruption, incessantly receive the favours of God, the time of harvest succeeding the season of gathering the grapes, and the season of gathering the grapes following the seed time, so that men, without any cessation or any interruption, are continually carrying home one crop and hoping for another, while one as it were lies in wait for the next; so that the beginnings of those which come on after are connected with the ends of those which have preceded them, and thus make a kind of circle and revolving body, which is endowed with every imaginable good. For the great multitude of things which are thus produced will be sufficient both for present use and enjoyment, and also for an unlimited abundance of supply in the time to come, the grain constantly coming up and flourishing, as the successors of the old, and filling up the void, which would otherwise be cursed by their decay and disappearance. There are also cases in which, by reason of the ineffable plenty, no one will think at all of those stores which have been collected long ago, but leaves them without any care or any attempt to store them, permitting every one who pleases to use them without restraint and with perfect impunity. For as to those men for whom that true wisdom is stored up, which has been derived from constant meditation and practice in wisdom and holiness, on them the wrath which consists of money upon earth is abundantly poured, since the treasure-houses, by the providence and care of God, are kept continually full; because the impulses of the mind, and the endeavours of the hands, are not hindered in any way, so as to prevent the successful attainment of these objects, which are constantly pursued with anxiety. But those persons who, by reason of their impiety or unrighteousness, have not a heavenly inheritance, have also no abundant possession or share of the good things upon the earth; and even if any such thing should come to them, it quickly departs again, as if it had originally happened to them, not for the advantage of the immediate recipients, but in order that a more vehement sorrow may overwhelm them, such as must, of necessity, follow the being deprived of an important blessing.

Chapter 18.

And at that time, says the law, you, by reason of the abundant fertility, shall do what you now suffer. For now, indeed, you pay no respect either to the laws or to the customs of your country and of your forefathers, but neglecting them altogether equally, you fail to obtain what is necessary, and keep counting the houses of the usurers and money-changers, being continually wishing to borrow at heavy interest; and then, as I said a minute ago, you shall do the contrary. For, by reason of your own unlimited abundance, you yourself shall lend to others, and that not lending little things, nor lending to few persons, but you shall lend large sums, and to many people, indeed to whole nations, all your affairs prospering and turning out well, both in the country and in the city; all things in the city, as respects offices of authority, and honour, and glory, and reputation, by means of wise conjectures, and prudent counsels, and conduct tending both in word and deed to the general advantage; and all the things in the country in consequence of the abundant production of all necessary things, such as corn, and wine, and oil, and all other productions which conduce to a comfortable and easy life, and these are the innumerable kinds of fruit from different trees, and the prolific increase of herds of oxen, and flocks of goats, and other kinds of cattle. But some one may say, What is the use of all these things to one who is not likely to leave heirs and successors behind him? The law, setting as it were the seal to its acts of beneficence, replies: No one shall be without offspring, nor shall there be a barren woman; but all the genuine and sincere servants of God shall fulfil the law of nature as respects the propagation of their species; or the men shall become fathers, and the fathers shall be happy in their offspring, and the women shall be happy mothers of children, so that every house shall be a full company of a numerous family, no part and no name being omitted of all those which are appropriated to relations, whether referring to relations upwards, such as uncles and grandfathers, or to descending relations on the other hand of a similar kindred, such as brothers, nephews, grandsons by the sons' side, grandsons by the daughters' side, cousins, counsins' children, and every kind of blood relations. But no man shall die prematurely or without having fulfilled the legitimate end of his being among those men who observe the laws, nor shall such fail to reach the age which God has allotted to the race of man. But the human being proceeding upwards from childhood, as it were by the different stages of a ladder, and at the appointed periods of time fulfilling the regularly determined boundaries of each age, will eventually arrive at the last of all, that which is near to death, or rather to immortality; being really and truly happy in his old age, leaving behind him a house happy in numerous and virtuous children in his own place.

Chapter 19.

This is what the lawgiver in one passage says, while declaring the will of God, that, "thou shalt complete the number of thy days," prophesying thus with great beauty and using great propriety and naturalness of language. For the man who is destitute of all learning, and who disregards the law, does not speak either in reason nor in number, as the old proverb says; but he who has a fair share of instruction and who adheres to the holy laws, receives as his first reward, since he is proved to be a respectable and reputable man, a share in number and arrangement. And very admirable is this fulness and completeness, not of months or years, but of days, so that no day whatever in the life of a virtuous man ever leaves an empty and open door for the entrance of sins, but is filled in all its parts and all its intervals with absolute virtue and excellence. For virtue and goodness are judged of not by quantity but by quality, for which reason I look upon it that even one day spent with perfect correctness is of equal value with the entire good life of a wise man. This is what is enigmatically implied in other expressions, where the holy writer says that such a man "shall deserve blessings both at his coming in and going out;" because the virtuous man is praiseworthy in all his positions and in all his actions, both indoors and out of doors, whether engaged in affairs of state or in the regulation of his household, regulating all his affairs inside his house with economy, and all the business out of doors with a due regard to principles of state government in the way in which it is most expedient for them to be regulated. If, then, any one proves himself a man of such a character in the city he will appear superior to the whole city, and if a city show itself of such a character it will be the chief of all the country around; and if a nation do so it will be the lord of all the other nations, as the head is to the body occupying the pre-eminence of situation, not more for the sake of glory than for that of advancing the interests of those that see. For continual appearances of good models stamp impressions closely resembling themselves on all souls which are not utterly obdurate and intractable; and I say this with reference to those who wish to imitate models of excellent and admirable beauty, that they may not despair of a change for the better, nor of an alteration and improvement from that dispersion, as it were, of the soul which vice engenders, so that they may be able to effect a return to virtue and wisdom. For when God is favourable every thing is made easy. And he is favourable to those who display modesty and due reverence, and who seek to pass over from intemperance to temperance, and who reproach themselves for all the blameable actions of their life, and for all the base images which they have stamped upon their polluted souls, and who aim at a tranquil state of the passions, and who keep constantly in view, as the proper object of their pursuit, a calmness and serenity of life. As therefore God, by one single word of command, could easily collect together men living on the very confines of the earth, bringing them from the extremities of the world to any place which he may choose, so also the merciful Saviour can bring back the soul after its long wandering, after it has been straying about in every direction, and been ill-treated by pleasure and desire, most imperious mistresses, and guide it easily from a trackless waste into a regular road when it has once determined to flee from evil without ever looking back, a flight not liable to reproach, but the cause of its preservation, which no one will do wrong to pronounce more desirable than any return.

Chapter 20.

These, then, of which we have already spoken, are what are called external goods, victory over one's enemies, superiority in war, confirmation of peace, and abundance of those good things which belong to peace, riches, and honours, and authorities, and the praises which always follow those who are successful, as they are extolled by every mouth both of friends and enemies, by the one through fear, and by the others out of good will. We must now proceed to speak of what is more nearly connected with us than these things, namely, about those things which affect the body. The lawgiver says, then, that a perfect freedom from disease in every respect, both privately and generally, shall be allotted to those persons who labour in the service of virtue and who make the sacred laws the guides of all their speeches and actions in life; and if there should any infirmity affect them it will not be for the sake of injuring them, but with a view to remind a mortal that he is mortal, so as to eradicate overbearing pride and improve his disposition. And sound health will follow, and a good condition of the outward senses, and a perfectness and completeness in all the parts, conducive to the unimpeded performance of those duties for which each man has been born. For God has thought fit to give as a reward to the virtuous a house thoroughly well built and well put together from the foundations to the roof; and the most natural house for the soul is the body, inasmuch as it does many things necessary and useful for life, and especially on account of the mind which has been purified by perfect purifications; and which, having been initiated in the divine mysteries, and having learnt to dwell only among the motions and periodical revolutions of the heavenly bodies, God has honoured with tranquillity, wishing it to be completely undisturbed and exempt from any contact of those passions which the necessities of the body engender, adding, out of covetousness, a desire for sovereignty over the passions. For either the heaven has caused a chill to something, or has scorched something, or has made something dry, or else, on the contrary, has melted and liquefied it; from all which causes the mind is unable to keep its path through life quite straight and independent. But if it has its abode in a healthy body, then it will with great care and tranquillity dwell among and devote all its leisure to the meditations of wisdom, having obtained a happy and fortunate existence. This is the mind which has drunk strong draughts of the beneficent power of God, and has feasted on his sacred words and doctrines. This is the mind in which the prophet says that God walks as in his palace; for the mind of the wise man is in truth the palace and the house of God. And he who is the God of all things is peculiarly called the God of this mind; and again this mind is by a peculiar form called his people, not the people of any particular rulers, but of the one only and true ruler, the Holy One of holies. This is the mind which a little while ago was enslaved to many pleasures and many desires, and to innumerable necessities arising from weaknesses and desires; but its evils God crushed in slavery, having elected to bring it to freedom. This is the mind which has received a favour not to be suppressed in silence, but rather to be proclaimed abroad and announced in every quarter, on account of the authority and power of its champion and defender, by which it was not thrust down to the tail, but was raised upwards to the head. but all these statements are uttered in a metaphorical form, and contain an allegorical meaning. For as in an animal the head is the first and best part, and the tail the last and worst part, or rather no part at all, inasmuch as it does not complete the number of the limbs, being only a broom to sweep away what flies against it; so in the same manner what is said here is that the virtuous man shall be the head of the human race whether he be a single man or a whole people. And that all others, being as it were parts of the body, are only vivified by the powers existing in the head and superior portions of the body. These are the prayers on behalf of good men who fulfil the laws by their actions which it is said will be accomplished by the grace of the bounteous and beneficent God, who honours and rewards all that is good for the sake of its similarity to himself. We must now consider the curses appointed against those who transgress the commandments and the Laws.

Chapter 21.

The lawgiver of our nation denounces the first curse as the lightest of evils, namely, poverty and indigence, and a want of all necessary things, and a participation in every kind of destitution; for, says he, "The enemy shall lay waste the corn-fields before they are ripe, and when the corn is ripened they shall suddenly come and reap it."{Deuteronomy 28:33.} Thus causing a twofold calamity, famine to their friends and abundance to their enemies; for the prosperity of one's enemies is more, or, at all events, not less painful than one's own misfortunes. And even if one's enemies are quiet, still those evils which proceed from nature and which are even more grievous, are not quiet; for you, indeed, sow the deep and fertile soil of the plain, but suddenly a cloud of locusts shall fly down and reap your crop, and what is left behind for you to carry home to your barns will bear but a very small proportion to what is sown. And, again, you shall plant a vineyard with unsparing expense, and incessant industry, and labour, such as it is natural for husbandmen to undergo; but when the vines are come to perfection, and are flourishing and weighed down with their own productiveness, the worms shall come and gather the grapes. And when you see your oliveyards flourishing, and an unbounded exuberance of fruit on the trees, you will very naturally be delighted from the hope of a successful harvest which you will be led to entertain, but when you begin to carry home the fruit, then you will be filled rather with sorrow than with joy; for the oil and all the fatness of the fruit will all flow away and disappear imperceptibly, and what is outside will be only a vain burden, empty, left only to deceive the empty soul. And, in short, all the seed crops and all the trees will be destroyed, fruit and all, by blight of one kind or another.

Chapter 22.

And there are other misfortunes also lying in wait for the men besides those which have been mentioned, all equally contributing to produce want and scarcity; for those things, by means of which nature used to provide men with good things, namely, the earth and the heaven, will both be rendered barren, the one being full of abortions and unable to bring any fruit to perfection, and the other changing its nature so as to produce an unproductive state of the seasons of the year, so that neither winter, nor summer, nor spring, nor autumn return in their appointed order, but are all violently wrenched from it, and thrown into a confusion destitute of all distinctive quality and completely disturbed, by the command of the supreme authority. For then there will be no rain, no showers, no gentle springs, no soft drops of moisture, no dew, nor anything else which can contribute to the growth of plants; but, on the contrary, all things which are calculated to dry them up when beginning to grow, all things destructive of the fruit when beginning to ripen, and adapted to prevent it from ever coming to perfection. For, says God, "I will make the heaven of brass for you, and the earth Iron."{Deuteronomy 28:23.} Implying by this enigmatical expression that neither of them shall accomplish the tasks which naturally belong to them and for which they were created; for how could iron ever bear ears of corn, or how could brass produce rain, of which all animals stand in need, and especially that animal so liable to misfortune and in need of so many things, man? And God intimates here not only barrenness and the destruction of the seasons of the year, but also the beginnings of wars, and of all the intolerable and ineffable evils which arise in wars; for brass and iron are the materials for warlike arms. And the earth, indeed, shall produce dust, and masses of dirt shall be brought down from above, from heaven, weighing down the fruit and destroying it by choking, in order that nothing may be omitted which can tend to complete destruction; for numerous families will be made desolate, and cities will suddenly become empty of their inhabitants, remaining as monuments of their former prosperity and records of subsequent disaster, for the warning of those who are capable of receiving correction.

Chapter 23.

And such a complete scarcity of all necessary things will seize the people that, being wholly destitute of and indifferent to them, they will turn even to devouring one another, eating not only the gentiles and those who are no relations to them, but even their nearest and dearest kinsfolk; for the father will take the flesh of his son, and the mother will eat of the life-blood of her daughter, brothers will eat their brothers, and children will devour their parents; and, in fact, the weaker will be continually the prey of the more powerful; and that wicked and accursed food, that of Thyestes, will seem to them like a joke when compared with the excessive and intolerable evils which their necessities bring upon them; for, as in the case of other persons, while they are in prosperity they desire length of life to be able to enjoy all good things, so also even those men overwhelmed with misery will have a vehement desire for life established in them, though it can only lead them to a participation in immoderate and interminable evils, all of which are likewise irremediable. For it would have been better for such men to have escaped misery by cutting off their griefs through death, which persons who are not utterly out of their senses are accustomed to do. But these men are arrived at such a degree of folly that they would be willing to live even to the longest possible time of life, being eager for and insatiably desirous of the greatest extremities of misery. Such evils, that which appears at first to be the lightest of all misfortunes, namely, poverty, is naturally calculated to produce, when it is the result of the vengeance of God; for even though cold, and thirst, and want of food may be terrible, still they might at times be objects worth being prayed for, if they only produced instantaneous death without any delay. But when they last a long time and waste away both body and soul, then they are calculated to reproduce the very greatest of the calamities recorded by the tragic poets, which appear to me to be described in a spirit of fabulous exaggeration.

Chapter 24.

Again. To free-born people slavery is a most intolerable evil, to avoid which wise men are willing even to die, resisting in a gallant spirit which despises all danger the attacks of those who seek to inflict upon them the domination of a master. Also, an invincible enemy is an intolerable evil. And if the same person be both things at once, namely, a master and an enemy, who can endure such a complication of calamities? For such a person will be possessed of the power of inflicting injury through his authority as a master, and he will be disinclined to pardon any one by reason of his irreconcileable enmity. Therefore the lawgiver pronounces that those persons who neglect the sacred laws shall have their enemies for their masters, who will treat them unmercifully, not only as having been reduced under their power by invincible attacks, but also as having voluntarily submitted to them through unforeseen calamities which famine and the want of necessaries has caused; for some persons think it well to choose lesser evils, if by so doing they can avoid greater ones; if, indeed, any one of the misfortunes above mentioned can be called a slight evil. Such men, becoming slaves, endure the services imposed on them by stern commands with their bodies, but when they are oppressed as to their souls with the anguish of still more bitter spectacles, they will sink under them; for they will see their enemies becoming the inheritors of houses which they have built, or of vineyards which they have planted, or of possessions which they have acquired, enjoying the good things and stores which have been prepared by others. And they will see their enemies feasting on the fattest of their cattle, and sacrificing them, and preparing them for the sweetest enjoyment, without being able to deprive those persons of anything who have thus robbed them. They will also see their wives, whom they married in holy wedlock for the purpose of propagating legitimate children, their modest, domestic, affectionate wives, insulted like so many courtesans. And they will rush forward to defend and to avenge them, but beyond resisting they will not be able to effect anything, being deprived of all their strength and utterly disabled; for they will be exposed as a mark for their enemies, an object for plunder, and ravage, and violence, and insult, and wounds, and injuries, and contumely, and utter destruction, so that nothing belong to them can escape, but no one dart of the enemy shall miss its blow, but every one of them shall be well aimed and successful. They shall be cursed in their cities and in their villages, and cursed in their town-houses and in their dwellings in the fields. Cursed will be their plains and all the seed which is sown in them; cursed will be the fertile soil of the mountain district, and all the kinds of trees which produce eatable fruit; cursed will be their herds of cattle, for they will be rendered barren and unproductive; cursed will be all their fruits and all their crops, for at the most critical period of their ripening they will be found to be all full of wind and destroyed. The storehouses full of food and money shall be made empty; no source of revenue shall be productive any more; all the arts, all the various businesses and employments, and all the innumerable varieties of life, shall be of no use to those who adopt them; for the hopes of those who are anxious shall fail to be fulfilled; and, in short, whatever they touch, in consequence of their wicked pursuits and wicked actions, the head, and front, and end of which is the abandonment of the service of God, shall all be vain and unprofitable.

Chapter 25.

For these things are the rewards of impiety and lawless iniquity. And, in addition to these things, there are diseases of the body which separately afflict and devour each limb and each part, and which also rack and torture it all over with fevers, and chills, and wasting consumptions, and terrible rashes, and scrofulous diseases, and spasmodic convulsions of the eyes, and putrefying sores and abscesses, and cutaneous disorders extending over the whole of the skin, and disorders of the bowels and inward parts, and convulsions of the stomach, and obstructions in the passages of the lungs preventing the patient from breathing easily, and paralysis of the tongue, and deafness of the ears, and imperfections of the eyes, and a general dimness and confusion of all the other senses, things which, though terrible, will yet hardly appear so when compared with other things more grievous still; when, for instance, all the vivifying qualities which existed in the blood contained in the veins have escaped from it, and when the breath which is contained in the lungs and windpipe is no longer capable of receiving a salutary admixture of the outward air so nearly connected with it; and when the veins are all relaxed and dissolved, which state is followed by a complete prostration of the harmony and due arrangement of the limbs, which were indeed previously distressed by the violent rush of a briny and very bitter stream stealthily pervading them; which, when it was shut up in a narrow passage having no easy outlet, being then pressed close and pressing other parts, conduces to the production of bitter and almost intolerable pains, from which are engendered the diseases of gout and arthritic pains and diseases, for which no salutary remedy has ever been discovered, but which are incurable by any human means. Some persons, when they behold these things, will be alarmed, marvelling to see how those who a little while ago were fat and full of good flesh, and flourishing exceedingly in health and vigour, have so on a sudden wasted away and become merely withered muscles and a thin skin; and how the women, formerly luxurious, and tender, and delicate by reason of the luxury to which they have been accustomed from their earliest infancy, now, from the terrible afflictions to which they have been subjected, have become wild in their souls, and wild-looking in their bodies. Then, then indeed, their enemies shall pursue them, and the sword shall exact its penalty; and they, fleeing to the cities, where they think that they have obtained a place of safety, being deluded by treacherous hopes, shall perish to a man being caught and destroyed by the ambuscades of their enemies.

Chapter 26.

And if, after all these calamities, they are not chastened, but still proceed by crooked paths, and turn off from the straight roads which lead to truth, then cowardice and fear shall be established in their souls, {Leviticus 26:36.} and they shall flee when no one pursues, and shall be routed and destroyed by false reports, as does often happen. The lightest sound of leaves falling through the air shall cause as great an agony of fear and apprehension as the most formidable war waged by the most powerful of enemies ought to produce, so that children shall be indifferent to the fate of their parents, and parents to that of their children, and brothers to that of their brethren, looking upon it that if they go to their assistance they may themselves incur the danger of captivity, while their best chance of safety consists in escaping by themselves. But the hopes of wicked men do never obtain their accomplishment, and those who hope to escape thus will be still more, or at all events not less, taken prisoners than those who were previously laid hold of. And even if some such persons do escape notice, they will still be exposed to insidious attacks from their natural enemies; and these are those most furious wild beasts who are well armed by the endowments of nature, and which God, simultaneously with the original creation of the universe, made for the purpose of striking terror into those men who were incapable of taking warning, and for executing implacable justice on those whose wickedness was incurable; and those who behold their cities razed to the very foundations will hardly believe that they were ever inhabited, and they will turn the sudden misfortunes which befall men after brilliant instances of prosperity into a proverb, recording all the instances which are mentioned or passed over in History. This contrast of present misery with former splendour is one of the circumstances mentioned by Thuycydides as enhancing the terrors of the disasters the Athenians met with in Sicily. There shall also come upon them asthmas, and consumptions affecting the internal organs, producing heaviness and despondency, with great afflictions, and making all life unstable, and hanging, as one may say, from a halter. And fears incessantly succeeding one another will toss the mind up and down, agitating it night and day, so that in the morning they shall pray for the evening, and in the evening they shall pray for the morning, on account of the visible horrors which surround them when awake, and the detestable images which present themselves to them in their dreams when sleeping. And the proselyte who has come over being lifted up on high by good fortune, will be a conspicuous object, being admired and pronounced happy in two most important particulars, in the first place because he has come over to God of his own accord, and also because he has received as a most appropriate reward a firm and sure habitation in heaven, such as one cannot describe. But the man of noble descent, who has adulterated the coinage of his noble birth, will be dragged down to the lowest depths, being hurled down to Tartarus and profound darkness, in order that all men who behold this example may be corrected by it, learning that God receives gladly virtue which grows out of hostility to him, utterly disregarding its original roots, but looking favourably on the whole trunk from its lowest foundation, because it has become useful and has changed its nature so as to become fruitful.

Chapter 27.

The cities being thus destroyed as if by fire, and the country being rendered desolate, the land will at last begin to obtain a respite, and, as one may say, to recover breath, and to look up again, after having been much exercised and harassed by the intolerable violence of its inhabitants, who drive away all the virgin periods of seven years out of the country, and discarded them from their minds; for nature taught men the only, or to speak more securely, the first festivals, namely, the recurring periods of seven days and seven years, making them times of rest, the seventh day being the period of rest for men, and the seventh year for the land. But these men, utterly disregarding the whole of this law, and violating all the obligations implied in salt, or treaties, or the altar of mercy, or the common hearth, considerations by which friendship and unanimity is usually cemented, for all such things are either the number seven itself, or exist in consequence of that number, oppressed (at least the more powerful of them did so) those men who were weaker with constant and uninterrupted commands, and they oppressed the land also, continually in their covetousness pursuing unrighteous gains, and inflaming their desires so as to excite their unbridled and unjust passions to an insatiable degree. For instead of granting to men who are in the truest point of view their brothers, as having one common mother, namely, nature, instead, I say, of giving them the appointed holiday after each period of six days, and instead of giving the land a respite after each space of six years without oppressing it either with sowing of seed or planting of trees, in order that it may not be exhausted by incessant labours: instead of acting thus, these men, neglecting all these admirable commandments, have oppressed both the bodies and souls of all men over whom they have had any power, with incessant severities, and have torn to pieces the strength of the deep-soiled earth, exacting revenues from it in an insatiable spirit beyond its power to contribute, and crushing it out altogether and in every part with exactions not only yearly, but even daily. For all which conduct, these men shall incur the penalties and curses mentioned above: and the country being thoroughly exhausted, and having been forced to submit to innumerable afflictions, shall at last be relieved by being delivered from the burden of its impious inhabitants, and when looking around it, shall see no one left of those who destroyed its grandeur and beauty, but shall behold the market-places all free from their tumults, and wars, and acts of iniquity, and full of tranquillity, and peace, and justice; then it shall recover its youth and former vigour, and shall enjoy tranquillity, and shall have rest at the festive seasons recurring at the sacred numbers of seven, recovering its strength again like an athlete who has been fatigued by his exertions. Then, like an affectionate mother, it shall pity the sons and the daughters whom it has lost, who now that they are dead are, and still more were, when alive, a grief and sorrow to their parents; and becoming young a second time, it will again be fertile as before, and will produce an irreproachable offspring, an improvement on its former progeny; for she that was desolate, as the prophet says, {Isaiah 54:1.} is now become happy in her children and the mother of a large family. Which prophetic saying has also an allegorical meaning, having reference to the soul; for when the family is very large, and the soul is full, all kinds of passions and vices, surrounding it like so many children, such for instance as pleasures, appetites, folly, intemperance, injustice, it is sad and diseased; and being exceedingly prostrate through illness, it is near to death, but when it is barren and has no such offspring, or when it has lost them, then it becomes changed in all its parts and becomes a pure virgin, and having received the divine seed, it fashions and brings to life a new family, very admirable in their nature, and of great beauty and perfection, such as prudence, courage, temperance, justice, holiness, piety, and all other virtues and good dispositions, of which not only is their birth a blessing accompanied by happiness in its children, but the mere expectation of such a birth is a blessing, since it cheers its weakness by the anticipations of hope; and hope is joy before joy, even though it may be somewhat defective in comparison with perfect joy. But still, it is in both these respects better than that which comes after; first, because it relaxes and softens the dry rigidity of care; and secondly, because by its anticipations it gives a forewarning of the impending perfect good.

Chapter 28.

I have now, then, without making any concealment of softening the truth in any degree, explained the curses and the punishments which it is fit for those persons to endure who have despised the sacred laws of justice and piety, and who have submitted themselves to the adoption of polytheistic opinions, the end of which is impiety through forgetfulness of the instruction originally imparted to them by their forefathers, which they learnt in their earliest infancy, when they were taught to look upon the nature of the One as the only supreme God, to whom alone those persons may properly be assigned as his inheritance who pursue the genuine truth instead of cunningly invented fables. If, however, they receive these exertions of power not as aiming at their destruction, but rather at their admonition and improvement, and if they feel shame throughout their whole soul, and change their ways, reproaching themselves for their errors, and openly avowing and confessing all the sins that they have committed against themselves with purified souls and minds, so as in the first place to exhibit a sincerity of conscience utterly alien from falsehood and concealing nothing evil beneath; and secondly, having their tongues also purified so as to produce improvement in their hearers, they will then meet with a favourable acceptance from their merciful saviour, God, who bestows on the race of mankind his especial and exceedingly great gift, namely, relationship to his own word; after which, as its archetypal model, the human mind was formed. For even though they may be at the very extremities of the earth, acting as slaves to those enemies who have led them away in captivity, still they shall all be restored to freedom in one day, as at a given signal; their sudden and universal change to virtue causing a panic among their masters; for they will let them go, because they are ashamed to govern those who are better than themselves.

Chapter 29.

But when they have received this unexpected liberty, those who but a short time before were scattered about in Greece, and in the countries of the barbarians, in the islands, and over the continents, rising up with one impulse, and coming from all the different quarters imaginable, all hasten to one place pointed out to them, being guided on their way by some vision, more divine than is compatible with its being of the nature of man, invisible indeed to every one else, but apparent only to those who were saved, having their separate inducements and intercessions, by whose intervention they might obtain a reconciliation with the Father. First of all, the merciful, and gentle, and compassionate nature of him who is invoked, who would always rather have mercy than punishment. In the second place, the holiness of all the founders of the nation, because they, with souls emancipated from the body, exhibiting a genuine and sincere obedience to the Ruler of all things, are not accustomed to offer up ineffectual prayers on behalf of their sons and daughters, since the Father has given to them, as a reward, that they shall be heard in their prayers. And, thirdly, that quality, on account of which above all others, the good will of the beings above-mentioned is conciliated, and that is the improvement and amelioration of those persons who are brought to treaties and agreements, who have, with great difficulty, been able to come from a pathless wilderness into a beaten road, the end of which is no other than that of pleasing God as sons please a father. And when they come cities will be rebuilt which but a short time ago were in complete ruins, and the desert will be filled with inhabitants, and the barren land will change and become fertile, and the good fortune of their fathers and ancestors will be looked upon as a matter of but small importance, on account of the abundance of wealth of all kinds which they will have at the present moment, flowing forth from the graces of God as from ever-running fountains, which will thus confer vast wealth separately on each individual, and also on all the citizens in common, to an amount beyond the reach even of envy. And the change in everything will be immediate, for God will nourish the virtues against the enemies of those who have repented, who have delighted in the ruined fortunes of the nation, reviling them, and making a mockery of them, as if they themselves were destined to have a season of good fortune, which could never be put an end to, which they hope to leave, in regular succession, to their children and to their posterity; thinking, at the same time, that they will for ever behold their adversaries in lasting and unchangeable misfortunes, laid up for even remote future generations; not perceiving, in their insanity, that they enjoyed that brilliant fortune which fell to their share a little while before, not for their own merits, but for the sake of giving a warning and admonition to others, for whom, as they had forsaken their national and hereditary customs, the only salutary remedy which could be found was the grief which they felt to excess when their enemies carried off their property. Therefore, weeping for and bewailing their own defeat, they will turn back again to the ancient prosperity of their ancestors, retracing all their steps with great exactness, and without its even happening to them to stray from the proper course and to be wrecked; but they who have turned their lamentations into ridicule, and have decided on celebrating, as public festivals, the days which they consider unlucky, and of feasting in memorial of matters for which they mourn, and who, in short, make themselves happy at all the unhappiness of others, when they begin to receive the due reward of their inhumanity, will learn that they have sinned, not against obscure and neglected persons, but against men of noble birth, having fuel to kindle their nobleness to a proper warmth, which, when it is properly fanned into a flame, then their glory, which a little while ago appeared to be extinguished, blazes out again. For as, when the trunk of a tree is cut down, if the roots are not taken away, new shoots spring up, by which the old trunk is again restored to life as it were;

in the very same manner, if there be only left in the soul ever so small a seed of virtue, when everything else is destroyed, still, nevertheless, from that little seed there spring up the most honourable and beautiful qualities among men; by means of which, cities, which were formerly populous and flourishing, are again inhabited, and nations are led to become wealthy and powerful.

www.ingramcontent.com/pod-product-compliance
Ingram Content Group UK Ltd.
Pitfield, Milton Keynes, MK11 3LW, UK
UKHW041903190726
13854UKWH00003B/1054